Turmeric Cookbook

Delicious & Healthy Turmeric Recipes

BY

Stephanie Sharp

License Notes

wwwwwwwwwwwwwwwwwwwwwwwwwwwwwwwwwwwwwwwwwww

My deepest thanks for buying my book! Now that you have made this investment in time and money, you are now eligible for free e-books on a weekly basis! Once you subscribe by filling in the box below with your email address, you will start to receive free and discounted book offers for unique and informative books. There is nothing more to do! A reminder email will be sent to you a few days before the promotion expires so you will never have to worry about missing out on this amazing deal. Enter your email address below to get started. Thanks again for your purchase!

Just visit the link or scan QR-code to get started!

https://stephanie-sharp.subscribemenow.com

wwwwwwwwwwwwwwwwwwwwwwwwwwwwwwwwwwwwwwwwww

Table of Contents

Introduction 9

Recipe 1: Fish Fillets with Lemon Turmeric Sauce 11

Recipe 2: Turmeric Marinated Chicken Wings 14

Recipe 3: Turmeric Raisin Rice 17

Recipe 4: Cauliflowers Roasted with Turmeric and Ginger
.... 20

Recipe 5: Turmeric Salad with Pumpkin and Sunflower
Seeds 22

Recipe 6: Mediterranean Golden Potatoes 25

Recipe 7: Spicy Turmeric Quinoa 28

Recipe 8: Turmeric Lemon Rice 31

Recipe 9: Roasted Red Snapper Smothered in Turmeric
.... 34

Recipe 10: Mejadra Pilaf 37

Recipe 11: Roasted Duck with a Turmeric and Plum Sauce

.... 40

Recipe 12: Rosemary Chicken made with Garlic and

Turmeric 44

Recipe 13: Turmeric Baby Zucchini Canoes 46

Recipe 14: Lemongrass and Turmeric Chicken 49

Recipe 15: Thai Basil and Turmeric Chicken Pasta 52

Recipe 16: Apricot Almond Barley Turmeric Salad 55

Recipe 17: Turmeric Chicken Tangy Wrap 58

Recipe 18: Stir-Fried Brussel Sprouts with Turmeric and

Cumin 61

Recipe 19: Pork Cutlets in Creamy Turmeric Sauce and

Cauliflower Rice 64

Recipe 20: Roasted Chickpea and Lentil Turmeric Salad

.... 68

Recipe 21: Broccoli and Turmeric Soup 71

Recipe 22: Kale Soup cooked with Turmeric and Banana

.... 74

Recipe 23: Beetroot, Apple and Turmeric Soup 77

Recipe 24: Creamy and Spicy Cauliflower Soup with

Turmeric 80

Recipe 25: Fennel, Leek and Walnut Soup with Turmeric

.... 83

Recipe 26: Lebanese Semolina Turmeric Cake 86

Recipe 27: Blueberry and Turmeric Muffins with Granola

on top 89

Recipe 28: Turmeric Almond Scones 93

Recipe 29: Orange, Turmeric and Greek Yoghurt Cake 96

Recipe 30: Turmeric Capsicum Cookies made with

Almond Walnut Meal 99

Conclusion 102

About the Author 103

Author's Afterthoughts.................................... 104

wwwwwwwwwwwwwwwwwwwwwwwwwwwwwwwwwwwwwwww

Introduction

Turmeric has been around since as early as 250 BC. It is essentially a golden-yellow root vegetable that is known to grow in the warmer temperatures. It carries a slightly bitter or peppery flavor and is often found in South Asian Curry dishes. In India it is also referred to as Indian Saffron due to the fact that it is often used as a substitute for actual saffron.

In terms of nutritional properties, it has been proven to portray antiviral, antibacterial, antitumor and anti-inflammatory potential. Due to this, turmeric has also been utilized as an organic remedy to assist in healing a variety of symptoms. One can turn to turmeric into home remedies for a large variety of chronic diseases. The main active compound in turmeric is curcumin which is also available as a supplement.

Recipe 1: Fish Fillets with Lemon Turmeric Sauce

A turmeric twist is added to this classic Lemon Butter fish recipe, giving it a creamier, full-bodied flavor on top of the sour elements contributed by the lemon. Elevate this dish with a side of boiled potatoes tossed with fresh thyme and a good pinch of salt and pepper.

Serves: 4

Cooking Time: 30 minutes

Ingredients:

- 4 Fish Fillets
- 2 Shallots
- 1 tsp. Turmeric
- 2 tbsp. unsalted Butter
- 16 spears of Asparagus
- ¾ to 1 cup of Heavy Cream
- Juice of half a Lemon
- 2 tbsp. of blanched, chopped lemon rind
- Coarse Salt and freshly ground White Pepper to taste

Directions:

1. Begin by slicing the fish fillets into 2 ½ inches by 1 ½ inches pieces. This should yield you four thin slices per fillet.

2. Then, start steaming the asparagus. In the meantime, sauté the shallots in the butter, followed by the fillets. Cook a few fillets at a time and cook until a light crust is formed. Proceed to carefully move the fish into a low-heated oven, which will help to slowly cook the fish and also keep it warm.

3. Drain the steamed asparagus, which should be cooked nicely by now.

4. Using the pan where the fish had been sautéed in, add in the lemon juice, turmeric and cream, and bring the ingredients to a boil. Take a peek at the fish fillets in the oven and add in any juices which may have collected in the tray.

5. Allow the sauce to simmer until thickened. Season with salt, pepper and the lemon rind.

6. Serve the fish fillets individually on plates with a generous slathering of sauce and a nice heap of asparagus.

wwwwwwwwwwwwwwwwwwwwwwwwwwwwwwwwwwwwwww

Recipe 2: Turmeric Marinated Chicken Wings

Turmeric is not only fantastic for flavor, but it works as a great anti-bacterial agent. Rubbing it into the mean will ensure that your fresh produce will be free from harmful microorganisms and bacteria. This turmeric recipe of chicken wings is Asian inspired, with other fragrant ingredients added in to complement the turmeric.

Serves: 8 wings

Cooking Time: 1 hour 25 minutes

Ingredients:

- 1stalk of fresh Lemongrass or 3 strips Lemon Zest, chopped
- 8 cloves of Garlic
- Freshly ground Black Pepper
- 3/4 cup of chopped Cilantro sprigs
- 1 tsp. Salt
- 1 tsp. Ground Turmeric
- 1 tbsp. Olive Oil
- 8 pieces of Chicken Wings

Directions:

1. Begin by trimming the lemongrass and slice them ¼ inches apart.

2. Add the lemongrass, cilantro, garlic, salt, turmeric and a good amount of ground black pepper and olive oil into a food processor.

3. Let the ingredients be blitzed until they are blended properly into a coarse paste.

4. Rub the mixture onto the chicken wings and let it refrigerate for a minimum of one hour, though letting them marinate overnight would really get the flavors to soak in.

5. When it is time to cook, heat up a grill to medium heat, which should be around 350 to 450 °F. Rub the grill with cooking oil before placing the chicken on it.

6. Let the meat cook for about 16 minutes and give it the occasional flip so it cooks evenly on both sides.

wwwwwwwwwwwwwwwwwwwwwwwwwwwwwwwwwwwwwww

Recipe 3: Turmeric Raisin Rice

A healthy and wholesome vegetarian rice dish cooked with "brain food" like turmeric and raisins. This simple meal can be prepared in a jiffy for last-minute parties or as a quick-and-easy date night meal for you and your other half!

Serves: 4-6

Cooking Time: 1 hour 15 minutes

Ingredients:

- 2 tsp. Coconut Oil
- ½ cup finely diced Onions
- 1 tsp. fresh Turmeric, grated
- 2 cloves of Garlic, grated
- 1 cup of short-grain Brown Rice
- ¼ cup of Golden Raisins
- 2 ½ cups of Vegetable Stock (or Water)
- Salt and Pepper to taste

Directions:

1. Begin by heating a saucepan to medium heat. Then, add in the coconut oil and toss in the onions once the oil starts heating. Sauté the onions for about 4 minutes, or until they are soft.

2. Combine in the raisins, turmeric, garlic and rice, toss the ingredients and allow them to sauté for about 2 more minutes.

3. Add in the stock/water. Cover the saucepan, reduce the heat and bring the ingredients to a boil. Allow it took cook until the rice is tender, which is about 45 minutes. To make the rice fluffy, remove the saucepan from the heat and let it steam for 5 minutes with the lid on.

4. Season the dish with enough salt or pepper before serving it while it's still steaming hot.

wwwwwwwwwwwwwwwwwwwwwwwwwwwwwwwwwwwww

Recipe 4: Cauliflowers Roasted with Turmeric and Ginger

Somehow, the crunchy goodness of cauliflowers seems to pop out more when cooked together with turmeric. This oven-roasted dish is a good way to entice children into eating their vegetable, and also the added bonus of having them be doused by the many good properties of turmeric. With a short preparation time, this dish can also be whipped up as a healthy midnight snack.

Serves: 4

Cooking Time: 35 minutes

Ingredients:

- 3 tbsp. of Vegetable Oil
- 1 tbsp. of freshly grated Ginger
- 1 head of Cauliflower, cut into bite-sized florets
- 1 tbsp. of Mustard Seeds (Black)
- 1 tsp. of Turmeric
- 1 Jalapeno, diced finely
- Salt and Pepper to taste

Directions:

1. Begin by preheating the oven to 425 °F.

2. Combine the turmeric, ginger, jalapeno, mustard seeds and oil in a small bowl, and give it a quick whisk.

3. In an appropriate-sized baking tray, toss the cauliflowers together with the flavored oil.

4. Season with enough salt and pepper before putting it into the oven.

5. Allow the cauliflowers to roast for about 20 minutes, or until they are lightly golden brown.

wwwwwwwwwwwwwwwwwwwwwwwwwwwwwwwwwwwwww

Recipe 5: Turmeric Salad with Pumpkin and Sunflower Seeds

The addition of turmeric to this recipe comes in the dressing, and it acts as a wonderful binding agent for all the vegetables added into this salad. Easy to whip up, this raw salad is definitely one that's going to spruce up your diet if you are a vegetarian or simply looking to eat healthy!

Serves: 2

Cooking Time: 25 minutes

Ingredients:

- ½ cup of Sweet Onion, chopped
- ¾ cup of Pumpkin Seeds
- ¾ cup of Sunflower Seeds
- 1 cup of chopped Celery
- 1 cup of chopped Cucumber
- 1 cup of Raisins
- 2 cups of chopped Jicama

Dressing:

- ¼ cup of Water
- ½ cup of Brazil Nuts
- 2 tsp. of Ground Turmeric
- 2 Dates

Directions:

1. Soak the pumpkin seeds and sunflower seeds overnight (roughly around 6 hours).

2. When beginning to prepare the salad, drain the seeds and rinse them thoroughly before placing them into a food processor.

3. Blitz them until they are coarsely chopped, then remove the seed and move them into your salad bowl.

4. Add in the rest of the ingredients and toss the salad.

Dressing:

1. Soak the dates and the Brazil nuts for about 3 hours.

2. Add the Brazil nuts, dates, turmeric and water into a blender and blend until smooth. Add into the salad and toss until all ingredients are integrated.

Recipe 6: Mediterranean Golden Potatoes

These potatoes look like they have been deep-fried to perfection, but don't be fooled! The trick of adding turmeric to the water in which the potato boils really gives it an electrifying yellow color. Bite into this beautiful salad and expect to find yourself nibbling on mustard seeds and cumin seeds, the ingredients that really give this recipe its Mediterranean edge.

Serves: 2

Cooking Time: 35 minutes

Ingredients:

- 1 lb. New Potatoes, skin on and cut into fingerling sizes
- ½ tsp. of toasted Mustard Seeds
- ½ tsp. of toasted Cumin Seeds
- ½ tsp. of Turmeric
- ½ tsp. of Salt
- 2 tbsp. of Olive Oil
- 3 tbsp. of Lemon Juice
- 6 grinds of freshly ground Pepper
- A handful of fresh Chives, chopped

Directions:

1. Add 6 cups of water into a pot and let it boil, whilst adding in 1 teaspoon of turmeric and 2 teaspoons of salt (not mentioned in the ingredients list above).

2. Boil the potatoes until they are tender and cool them down with ice water, for handling purposes. Transfer the potatoes into a salad bowl.

3. Bring together the olive oil, lemon juice, garlic, salt, turmeric and black pepper. Whisk them lightly.

4. Add the dressing, mustard seeds, cumin seeds and chives to the potatoes. Toss them while they are still warm so the dressing gets absorbed properly.

5. Cover the salad and refrigerate them or eat it while it's still warm.

wwwwwwwwwwwwwwwwwwwwwwwwwwwwwwwwwwwwww

Recipe 7: Spicy Turmeric Quinoa

We all love quinoa and its pseudo-cereal property. Is it rice, or is it cereal, or is it a weird representation of an in-between? Whatever it is, this superfood is loaded with protein, fiber and minerals, which helped boost quinoa's fame. Known to be loaded with anti-inflammatory and anti-oxidant phytonutrients, quinoa is the choice of rice substitute for those who watch their weight and is the protein substitute for vegans.

Serves: 4

Cooking Time: 25 minutes

Ingredients:

- ½ tsp. of Cumin Seeds
- ½ tsp. of Mustard Seeds
- ½ tsp. Ground Turmeric
- ½ cup of frozen Green Peas
- ½ cup of Grape Tomatoes, halved
- 1 cup of Quinoa
- 1 chopped Onion
- 1 tsp. Salt
- 2 tbsp. of Vegetable Oil
- 2 tbsp. of Lemon Juice
- 2 cloves of Garlic, minced

Directions:

1. Begin by rinsing the quinoa, drain and set aside.

2. Pour the vegetable oil into a saucepan and fry the onion, garlic, cumin and mustard seeds for 2 minutes.

3. Then, add in the quinoa and turmeric. Stir to combine the flavors.

4. Add in 2 cups of water and add salt when the water begins to boil. Reduce the heat and cover the saucepan, letting the quinoa to cook for about 12 minutes.

5. Add in the frozen green peas, and if the quinoa looks too dry, add in a tablespoon or two of water. Allow it to cook for a couple of minutes, or until all the water is absorbed. Cooked quinoa should look be soft and translucent.

6. Lastly, add in the tomato halves as well as the lemon juice, and give the quinoa a nice mix.

wwwwwwwwwwwwwwwwwwwwwwwwwwwwwwwwwwwwww

Recipe 8: Turmeric Lemon Rice

Enjoy this delicious Turmeric Lemon Rice with some groundnuts and lentils for a delicious dinner or on its own as a tasty snack.

Serves: 4

Cooking Time: 30 minutes

Ingredients:

- 1 ½ cup of Rice
- 1 tbsp. of freshly grated Ginger
- ½ tsp. of Ground Turmeric
- 1 tsp. of Salt
- ½ cup of Split Peas (yellow)
- 1 tbsp. of black Mustard Seeds
- 2 tbsp. of Oil
- Coriander leaves, 2 tbsp., chopped
- Red Chili, 2 tbsp., dried
- Lemon juice, 4 tbsp.
- Water, 3 cups
- Unsalted Peanuts

Directions:

1. Wash the rice and soak it for about 15 minutes and do the same with the dal.

2. Add your water to a deep pan and allow to boil. Water level should be ½ an inch above the rice.

3. Add the soaked rice and cover the pan, letting the rice simmer on a low-medium heat.

4. Once the rice is cooked (15 minutes), turn off the heat and let it rest for 5 minutes. After that, fluff up the rice and keep it aside.

5. Combine your turmeric, salt and lemon juice then set aside.

6. Allow the oil to get hot then add in your red chili and mustard seeds. Reduce the heat as the mustard seeds begin to pop, add in your drained dal, turmeric mixture and lemon juice.

7. Let it simmer for a couple of minutes while stirring occasionally. Then, add in the cooked rice, grated ginger and the peanuts. Continue stirring gently for 1 minute.

8. Scoop the rice onto a plate and garnish with fresh coriander before serving it up.

wwwwwwwwwwwwwwwwwwwwwwwwwwwwwwwwwwwwwww

Recipe 9: Roasted Red Snapper Smothered in Turmeric

This delicious Snapper is amazingly easy to whip up and is incredibly tasty.

Serves: 4

Cooking Time: 55 minutes

Ingredients:

- Red Snapper, 3.5 lbs., whole, gutted, scaled and lightly slashed
- Lime, 4 slices
- Kaffir Lime leaves, a handful
- Some slices of Galangal root
- A mix of Basil and Mint, about a handful
- Some slices of Lemongrass
- Turmeric, ground, 1 tsp.
- White Peppercorns, 1 tsp., whole
- Cilantro roots and stems, 1 tsp., chopped
- Garlic, 3 ½ tsp., peeled
- A good pinch of salt
- 2 tbsp. of vegetable oil

Directions:

1. Set your oven to preheat to 400°F.

2. Add your cilantro roots, peppercorns and turmeric to a grinder then process. Add in the salt and vegetable oil and mix the ingredients.

3. Use the turmeric paste you created to cover both sides of your fish (ensure to get it into the slashed sections).

4. Stuff your fish with your lime slices and herbs, then set to bake until flaky (about 35 minutes).

Recipe 10: Mejadra Pilaf

Pilaf (also known as pilau or polo) refers to rice dishes which are cooked in a broth that can be seasoned with spices, meat, vegetables or all of them together. This recipe is just done with spices but if you'd like, you could always add in some meat stock or accompany this vegetarian rice dish with a meat dish!

Serves: 4

Cooking Time: 30 minutes

Ingredients:

- 2 tbsp. Olive Oil
- 2 tsp. Cumin Seeds
- 1 ½ tsp. of Ground Turmeric
- 1 ½ of Coriander seeds
- 1 ½ tsp. of ground Cinnamon
- 1 ¼ cup of Water
- 1 tsp. Sugar
- 1 tsp. Salt
- 1 cup of Basmati Rice
- I tin of lentils (14oz), drained
- ½ cup of crunchy Asian fried shallots
- Black Pepper to taste

Directions:

1. Heat up olive oil in a saucepan over medium heat before adding in the cumin seeds and coriander seeds.

2. Let the spices cook for a couple of minutes until it is fragrant.

3. Add in the rice and toss that with the oil and spices for a few minutes.

4. Then, add in the water and the lentils.

5. When the concoction begins to boil, add in all the other spices alongside with the salt and pepper.

6. Turn down the heat to medium-low and cover the saucepan with a lid to let the rice cook for 10 to 12 minutes, or until most of the liquid have been absorbed.

7. After that, remove the saucepan from heat source and let the rice rest for 10 minutes.

8. Right before serving, add in the fried shallots and stir once more. Adjust the salt and pepper if needed, and garnish with some more shallots and some coriander. Add a scoop of yoghurt on the side, if desired.

wwwwwwwwwwwwwwwwwwwwwwwwwwwwwwwwwwwwwww

Recipe 11: Roasted Duck with a Turmeric and Plum Sauce

Looking for something else to serve during Thanksgiving instead of good ol' turkey? Well, how about Chinese-inspired roasted duck? Duck and plum are two ingredients that are popular in the Chinese cuisine. Although this dish may not radiate the yellow color of turmeric but more of the purple from the plums, you would still be able to taste the presence of turmeric and the amazing way it enhances flavors.

Serves: 4

Cooking Time: 2 hours 40 minutes

Ingredients:

Turmeric and Plum Sauce:

- 12 plums, pitted and quartered
- 2 inches of Turmeric Root, or 1 ½ tsp. of Ground Turmeric
- 1 cup of Water
- 1 tsp. of Honey
- 1 clove of Garlic, minced
- 3 Pearl Onions, chopped
- ⅛ cup of Butter or Ghee

Roasted Duck:

- 1 duck
- ¼ cup of Salt
- ⅓ cup of Olive Oil
- ½ cup of Orange Juice
- 4 to 6 sprigs of Rosemary

Directions:

1. Begin preparing the duck by removing its organs, if needed.

2. Break the rosemary sprigs to release the flavors and add it into a Ziplock bag together with the olive oil, orange juice and the salt. Shake up the ingredients until they are integrated.

3. Add in the duck, squeeze out the air and let it sit in the fridge for about 1 ½ to 2 ½ hours.

4. When you are going to roast the duck, preheat the oven to 325°F. Line the roasting pan with the rosemary sprigs and lay the duck in, breast up. Let it roast for about 60 to 80 minutes, until the skin is brown and crispy. If you are using a meat thermometer, the internal temperature of the duck should be at 165°F.

5. To begin preparing the sauce, add ghee into a saucepan, and then add in the plums and sauté them.

6. Grate the turmeric into the saucepan, alongside the garlic and pearl onions. Sauté the ingredients until they are soft.

7. Add in the honey and water and allow the dish to simmer for about 60 minutes until it reaches a thick texture, almost ketchup-like.

wwwwwwwwwwwwwwwwwwwwwwwwwwwwwwwwwwwwwwww

Recipe 12: Rosemary Chicken made with Garlic and Turmeric

This is a deliciously healthy dish, if you don't mind the rather strong garlic breath that may follow after. Next to turmeric, garlic is also known for its many health benefits, as it is used to treat conditions of the heart and blood, to combat cancer and acts as an anti-bacterial that can possibly kill off E.coli and Salmonella bacteria in the stomach.

Serves: 3

Cooking Time: 30 minutes

Ingredients:

- 1 lb. of Chicken breasts, chunked
- 1 Lemon and its Zest
- 7 cloves of Garlic, minced
- 1 ½ tbsp. of ground Rosemary
- 2 tsp. of Ground Turmeric
- 5 tbsp. of Olive Oil
- Sea Salt and Pepper to taste

Directions:

1. Marinate the chicken in all of the ingredients for a couple of hours, or overnight if you have the time.

2. When ready to prepare, preheat the oven to 374 °F.

3. Place the marinated chicken in an oven-friendly dish and let it bake for 15 to 20 minutes. Stir occasionally to ensure that chicken is cooked evenly.

4. Serve with a vegetable dish of choice.

Recipe 13: Turmeric Baby Zucchini Canoes

We all know that getting children to eat their vegetables can be quite a challenge. The vitamins and minerals are vital for their growth, even though they may not really understand that. This recipe can help you solve that problem, because which child would not like ground meat?

Serves: 6

Cooking Time: 35 minutes

Ingredients:

- 6 Baby Zucchinis
- ¼ cup of Coconut Oil (or Bacon Fat)
- 1 chopped Onion
- 6 sliced Mushrooms
- 2 lbs. ground Meat of choice
- 1 thumb of Ginger, minced
- 1 thumb of Turmeric, minced
- 1 zest of a Lemon
- Salt to taste

Directions:

1. Begin by preheating the oven to 350°F.

2. Fry the onions in one tablespoon of oil or fat until it is golden brown. Add the rest of the ingredients into the pan and stir occasionally until the meat is cooked.

3. In the meantime, cut the zucchinis lengthwise and slice out the seeds to make a cavity in each of the zucchini 'canoe.'

4. Lay the halves close to each other on a baking tray with the cut side facing upwards. Brush them with the remaining oil or fat and fill them up with the meat mixture. You don't have to be neat and precise when filling it up, just remember to be generous with the protein!

wwwwwwwwwwwwwwwwwwwwwwwwwwwwwwwwwwwwwww

Recipe 14: Lemongrass and Turmeric Chicken

The flavors of turmeric and lemongrass go together like peanut butter and jelly, and lemongrass has its fair share of healthy properties too. Like turmeric, lemongrass is also known to have antimicrobial, antioxidant, anti-inflammatory and anti-cancer properties. Serve it with a portion of rice cooked with some turmeric and you'll have a meal that's Turmerifically true in nature and appearance too!

Serves: 4-6

Cooking Time: 1 hour 10 minutes

Ingredients:

- 1¼ cup of canned unsweetened Coconut Milk
- 3 Shallots or 1 medium Onion, minced
- 2 Lemongrass stocks, finely chopped (do remove the tougher outer layers as you reach the last third of the lemongrass)
- 1-2 Jalapenos, seeded and minced
- 1 tbsp. of Curry Powder
- 1 to 2 tbsp. of grated Ginger
- 1 to 2 tbsp. of freshly grated Turmeric
- 3 tbsp. of freshly squeezed Lime Juice
- Zest of one Lime
- 1 tbsp. of Fish Sauce
- 1 tbsp. of Coconut Aminos
- 3 to 4 lbs. of Chicken leg and thigh pieces
- Chopped Cilantro

Directions:

1. Aside from the chicken and the cilantro, combine all the ingredients and blend them in a blender.

2. Lay out the chicken pieces in a baking dish and douse it with the blended sauce. Leave it in the fridge to marinate overnight.

3. When ready to cook, preheat the oven to 350°F and remove the chicken from the fridge.

4. Let the chicken bake for about 50 minutes or until meat is tender enough to be separated easily from the bone.

5. Serve with turmeric rice and garnish with the chopped cilantro.

Recipe 15: Thai Basil and Turmeric Chicken Pasta

If you've grown tired of your Carbonaras and Marinaras, then you should give this recipe a chance. For starters, the pasta for this dish is not really pasta, its zucchini made into thin spaghetti-like strips! Far from the standard Italian pasta flavors, this one is definitely made for the turmeric to shine.

Serves: 4

Cooking Time: 45 minutes

Ingredients:

- 1.5 lbs. of Chicken
- 1 can of Coconut Milk
- 3 Zucchini
- ⅓ cup of freshly chopped Basil Leaves
- ½ tsp. of Cayenne Pepper
- 1 tbsp. of Apple Cider Vinegar
- 1 ½ tsp. of ground Ginger or freshly grated Ginger
- 2 tsp. of ground Turmeric
- 2 ½ tsp. of Sea Salt
- 2 tsp. of Garlic Powder or some cloves of fresh Garlic
- 3 tbsp. of Coconut Palm Sugar

Directions:

1. Begin by cutting the chicken into small chunks that are bite-sized and appropriate for a pasta meal.

2. Make the zucchini noodles with a spiralizer.

3. In a large saucepan, turn the heat on high and add 2 tablespoon of coconut oil and toss in the chicken. Cook until it's no longer pink and add in the zucchini noodles.

4. Add in the spices and stir again, letting it cook for a while.

5. Pour in the coconut milk over the dish, add the apple cider vinegar and stir everything again.

6. Let the whole dish cook for another 10 minutes on medium heat or until chicken is fully cooked. Enjoy!

wwwwwwwwwwwwwwwwwwwwwwwwwwwwwwwwwwwwww

Recipe 16: Apricot Almond Barley Turmeric Salad

For a turmeric filled salad that is perfect for either lunch or a heavier snack, give this recipe a go.

Serves: 10-12

Cooking Time: 1 hour 15 minutes

Ingredients:

- ½ tsp. ground Turmeric
- Water, 4 ½ cups
- Nutmeg, ground, 1 pinch
- Salt, ½ tsp.
- Parsley, 2 tbsp., chopped
- Cinnamon, ½ tsp., ground
- Honey, 2 tbsp.
- Pearl Barley, 1 ½ cups
- Apricots, 1 cup, dried, sliced
- Almonds, 1 cup, slivered, blanched
- Yogurt, 1 cup, Plain
- Lemon, 1, juiced
- Canola Oil, 1 tbsp.
- Red Onion, 1, thinly sliced

Directions:

1. Rinse your barley. And then, bring water to a boil in a saucepan. Add in the barley, stir and let it boil.

2. Cover the pan and reduce the heat, let the barley simmer for about 45 minutes or until water is absorbed.

3. Add your oil into a pan on medium heat and allow to get hot. Add in the onion and let it sauté until it is golden brown.

4. Toss together your parsley, almonds, apricots, fried onions, and barley.

5. In another small bowl, mix in the salt, nutmeg, turmeric, cinnamon, honey, lemon juice, and yoghurt. Mix them together until they are integrated.

6. Combine the mixture with your barley mixture then toss to combine.

7. Preferably served at room temperature, to mellow out the flavors.

Recipe 17: Turmeric Chicken Tangy Wrap

Wraps are a wonderful meal-in-one that you can carry around easily. Perfect for when you want to add a twist to a barbeque session. Keep leftover chicken and make them as a bring-in-your-own-lunch meal at work or as a healthy (and affordable) post-workout meal.

Serves: 4

Cooking Time: 35 minutes

Ingredients:

- 1 cup of Plain Yoghurt
- I medium Cucumber, diced
- 1 Chicken breast, skinless and boneless, and cut into strips
- 1 bunch of Parsley, chopped finely
- 2 tbsp. of Lemon Juice
- 4 Tortillas
- ½ an Onion, chopped
- 1 tbsp. of ground Turmeric
- 1 tsp. of Vegetable Oil
- ½ tsp. of Paprika
- ½ tsp. of Salt
- ¼ tsp. of ground Cumin
- ¼ cup of Water
- ⅛ tsp. of Cayenne Pepper
- ⅛ tsp. of ground Ginger
- Ground Black Pepper to taste

Directions:

1. Begin by whisking the yoghurt, lemon juice, turmeric, onion, cumin, salt, ginger, paprika, cayenne pepper and black pepper in a ceramic bowl.

2. Add in the chicken and toss it so it's evenly coated. Cover the bowl with cling wrap and let it marinate in the fridge for a minimum of an hour.

3. Preheat an outdoor grill onto high heat and lightly oil the grill. Cook the chicken on the grill until it is nicely brown and most importantly, no longer pink in the middle.

4. This should take about 5 to 7 minutes. Cut the chicken into bite sized pieces.

5. In a small saucepan, pour in the water, oil and remaining marinade and bring it to a boil over a high heat.

6. Switch the heat to low, then allow the mixture to simmer until thickens, which should take about 10 minutes. Add in the chicken and stir.

7. Serve chicken on the tortillas and top it with the cucumber and parsley, and tuck in!

wwwwwwwwwwwwwwwwwwwwwwwwwwwwwwwwwwwwwwww

Recipe 18: Stir-Fried Brussel Sprouts with Turmeric and Cumin

These mini-cabbages taste wonderful when cooked up in this style. They're wonderful to beaten on their own, paired with a rice and curry dish or as a 'slaw substitute in hot dogs. The turmeric yellow complements the lovely green color of the Brussel sprouts and biting into little bits of mustard seeds release earthy flavors that works well with the cumin.

Serves: 2

Cooking Time: 25 minutes

Ingredients:

- 10 Brussel Sprouts
- 2 tbsp. of Olive Oil
- ½ tsp. of ground Turmeric
- ½ tsp. of Cumin Seeds
- ½ tsp. of Mustard Seeds
- 1 small Onion, chopped
- 4 Garlic cloves, chopped
- 2 Green Chilies, sliced lengthwise
- 5 to 7 Curry Leaves

Directions:

1. Begin by slicing up the Brussel sprouts into nice, thin slices and put it into a bowl.

2. Then, add in the turmeric powder, some garlic, onions, green chilies and salt, and stir until all the ingredients are combined.

3. In a skillet, heat up the olive oil and add in the mustard seeds. When the seeds begin to pop, add in the cumin seed and the rest of the garlic.

4. Sauté the ingredients for about 2 minutes, and then add in the Brussels mixture.

5. Cook them for about 5 to 8 minutes, but make sure the Brussel sprouts don't lose their green color.

wwwwwwwwwwwwwwwwwwwwwwwwwwwwwwwwwwwwwwwwww

Recipe 19: Pork Cutlets in Creamy Turmeric Sauce and Cauliflower Rice

Sometimes, the key to a wonderful meat dish is the sauce and in this recipe, the sauce is definitely the highlight. Made with coconut milk as the base instead of cream, this sauce is made to be more Asian with the added ingredient of fish sauce. Although an uncanny combination, who can deny it when flavors mix and merge beautifully! This dish is also best served with a side of buttered cauliflower rice.

Serves: 4

Cooking Time: 40 minutes

Ingredients:

Creamy Sauce:

- 2 tbsp. of freshly squeezed Lime juice
- 2 Garlic Cloves
- 1 tbsp. of Fish Sauce
- 1 tsp. of Turmeric
- 1 small Jalapeno, roughly chopped
- 13.5oz of Coconut Milk
- Handful of Cilantro leaves

Pork:

- 4 boneless Pork Cutlets or ½ inch thin Pork Chops
- 1 tbsp. of Coconut Oil
- 1 shallot, finely chopped
- Salt and Turmeric for seasoning

Cauliflower Rice:

- 1 head of Cauliflower
- Enough Butter to taste
- Enough Salt to taste

Directions:

1. Add in coconut milk, garlic, lime juice, fish sauce, jalapeno, 1 teaspoon turmeric, and the cilantro in a blender, and blend the ingredients till it forms a smooth sauce.

2. Season the pork with enough salt and turmeric.

3. Add coconut oil into a skillet and sauté the shallots for 30 seconds.

4. Cook the thin pork cutlets/pork chops for about 2 minutes on each side or until they are lightly browned.

5. Remove the pork from the skillet and add the coconut sauce in. Boil the sauce for 5 minutes.

6. Begin to prepare the cauliflower rice by trimming and roughly chopping up the cauliflower head.

7. Either grate the cauliflower by hand or blitz it in a food processor until the cauliflower obtains the texture of rice.

8. Sauté the cauliflower in a pan with some oil until it is soft, which should take about 5 to 10 minutes. Season sufficiently with butter and salt.

9. Then, add the pork and its juices into the coconut sauce, and allow it to simmer just long enough to heat up the pork.

10. The creamy pork is ready to be served with the cauliflower rice. Make it look even more appealing by garnishing it with chopped cilantro.

wwwwwwwwwwwwwwwwwwwwwwwwwwwwwwwwwwwwww

Recipe 20: Roasted Chickpea and Lentil Turmeric Salad

This is a delicious salad that would be perfect for a picnic.

Serves: 3

Cooking Time: 40 mins.

Ingredients:

- Chickpeas, 15.5oz, canned, rinsed
- Brown Lentils, 8oz, dried
- Chicken Stock, 2 cups
- Flat-Leaf Parsley, 2 tbsp., chopped
- Canola Oil, 1 tsp.
- Garlic, 1 clove, smashed
- Bay Leaf, 1
- Lemon, 1, halved
- Yellow Onion, 1 small, halved
- Kosher Salt, ½ tsp.
- Turmeric, ½ tsp., ground
- Black Pepper, ¼ tsp., ground
- Cumin, ¼ tsp., ground
- Red Bell Peppers, ¼ cup, roasted, chopped

Directions:

1. Set your oven to preheat to 375°F. In an oven-friendly dish, add the chickpeas, oil, salt, turmeric, pepper and cumin and toss it.

2. Spread the mixture evenly and allow it to bake for about 45 minutes until golden brown.

3. In the meantime, boil the chicken stock over a high heat in a saucepan. Add in a half of your lemon, bay leaf, onion, garlic, and lentils.

4. Set your lentils to cook until tender (about 20 minutes). Toss your bay leaf, onion, garlic, and lemon.

5. In a medium bowl, toss the chickpeas, lentils, bell pepper and parsley.

6. Add the juice of the remaining half of the lemon and toss until ingredients combine properly.

Recipe 21: Broccoli and Turmeric Soup

Broccoli is a delicious vegetable to turn into soup, if you know how to combine it with the right ingredients. Turmeric added into this soup helps to elevate the green vegetable's flavor and bring it to new heights. A squeeze of lemon juice is what's needed to give this creamy soup the tangy touch it needs.

Serves: 4

Cooking Time: 50 minutes

Ingredients:

- 1 large head of Broccoli
- ½ a cup of diced White Onion
- ½ a Lemon
- 2 cloves of Garlic, minced
- 1 stalk of Celery, diced
- 1 tbsp. of organic virgin Coconut Oil
- 1 tsp. of ground Turmeric
- 1 Bay Leaf
- 1 small Avocado
- ¼ tsp. of grated fresh Ginger
- ⅛ tsp. of freshly ground Black Pepper
- ⅛ tsp. of Cayenne Pepper
- 5 cups of Vegetable Stock
- 1 ½ tsp. of Himalayan Pink Salt

Directions:

1. First, melt the coconut oil in a large pot over medium heat. Then, add in the celery and onions, and sprinkle the ingredients with 1 teaspoon of the salt. Cook them for 3 minutes, until they are soft.

2. Toss in the garlic and turmeric and continue cooking for another 2 minutes. Continue cooking on low heat while stirring.

3. Add in the broccoli florets, vegetable stock, ginger, bay leaf, cayenne, black pepper and the rest of the salt.

4. Cover the pot and cook the broccoli on a medium-low heat until the broccoli is tender, which would be 25 to 30 minutes.

5. After that, remove the ingredients from the heat and toss in the peeled and pitted avocado. Puree the soup with a hand blender and add in more salt if needed.

6. Pour the soup into bowls and squeeze a bit of lemon juice before serving.

wwwwwwwwwwwwwwwwwwwwwwwwwwwwwwwwwwwwwww

Recipe 22: Kale Soup cooked with Turmeric and Banana

What a strange combination of ingredients, don't you think? Nonetheless, the content of the soup seem to gel well with each other. This soup is a truly a power blend, with lots of health-helping ingredients like sweet potatoes, kale, turmeric, ginger, garlic and bananas.

Serves: 6

Cooking Time: 40 minutes

Ingredients:

- 3 cups of Carrots, cut into large chunks
- 10 cups of Kale, julienned
- 2 tbsp. of freshly grated Ginger
- 3 large Sweet Potatoes
- 3 stalks of Celery cut into large chunks
- 3 cloves of Garlic
- 2 large Bananas cut into thin slices
- 1 large Onion, cut into quarters
- 1 leek, cut into large chunks
- 1 tbsp. of Turmeric
- ¾ cup of Cashew Butter
- Juice of 1 or 2 Lemons
- 10 cups of Water
- Freshly ground Black Pepper to taste
- Sea Salt to taste

Directions:

1. In a large soup pot, add in the water, turmeric, ginger, onions, sweet potatoes, carrots, leek, celery, and garlic.

2. Add in a teaspoon of salt and let the vegetables cook on medium heat until tender.

3. In a small bowl, place the sliced bananas with lime juice and set aside.

4. Once the vegetables are done, remove from heat and blend them together with the broth.

5. The idea is to create a thin soup, so add more filtered water is necessary.

6. Add in the cashew butter and mix the soup. Return to heat and toss in the chopped kale. Let it cook until the kale is tender.

7. Add salt to taste. When serving the soup, place some of the sliced bananas that had been soaking in lime juice.

8. Top it with a sprinkling of black pepper.

Recipe 23: Beetroot, Apple and Turmeric Soup

This is a really simple soup to make and it is jam-packed with a lot of vitamins. Just a little word of advice; this soup is made with not one, but TWO stain-crazy vegetables. The soup looks brilliant with its deep purple hue, but it will stain almost anything and everything!

Serves: 4

Cooking Time: 50 minutes

Ingredients:

- 4 Baby Onions, diced
- 4 cups of good quality Vegetable Stock
- 3 Celery sticks and its leafy tops, chopped
- 2 tbsp. of Sunflower Oil
- 2 large, organic Beetroot, scrubbed and cubed
- 2 organic Red Apples, cored and cubed
- 2 cups of Water
- 1 tsp. of ground Cumin
- 1 tsp. of freshly grated organic Turmeric root
- ¼ tsp. of ground Cinnamon

Directions:

1. In a deep saucepan, heat the oil over medium heat. Add in the onions and celery sticks (only) and cook until the onion is translucent and soft.

2. Put in the ground cumin and cinnamon, and stir the ingredients until fragrant, while keeping the heat on medium.

3. Throw in the beetroot, apple and the turmeric. Toss the ingredients for a couple of minutes and increase the heat.

4. Add the celery leafy tops, the vegetable stock and water. Bring the ingredients to a simmer.

5. Reduce the heat and let the soup simmer until the beetroot is tender, which is about 35 minutes.

6. Remove the pot from the heat and blend the ingredients in the pot until the soup is smooth.

7. Return to the heat and when ready to serve, top the serving with a squeeze of lemon juice.

wwwwwwwwwwwwwwwwwwwwwwwwwwwwwwwwwwwwwww

Recipe 24: Creamy and Spicy Cauliflower Soup with Turmeric

Enjoy this luxurious-tasting cauliflower soup, and with the addition of all the right spices including turmeric, it is nothing short of healthy and bursting with flavors. One slurp will quickly multiply into 10 and before you know it, you're on your third bowl! Fret not though. Have as much as you want for this is one healthy, delicious soup.

Serves: 6

Cooking Time: 30 minutes

Ingredients:

- 4 ½ cups of Vegetable Broth
- 1 large head of Cauliflower, roughly chopped
- 4 cloves of Garlic, minced
- 2 Yellow Onions, diced
- 1 tbsp. Apple Cider Vinegar
- 1 tbsp. of Coconut Oil or Olive Oil
- 1 Bay Leaf
- 1 cup of Coconut Milk (canned or fresh)
- 1 ¼ tsp. ground Cumin
- 1 tsp. of ground Turmeric
- 1 tsp. of Kosher Salt
- ½ tsp. ground Coriander
- ⅛ tsp. of ground Cardamom
- A dash of ground Black Pepper
- A dash of Red Pepper Flakes, crushed
- Fresh Dill for garnish

Directions:

1. Heat the oil over medium-heat in a large pot. Add in the onions, cumin, bay leaf, turmeric, coriander, cardamom, black pepper, crushed red flakes and kosher salt.

2. Sauté the ingredients and stir occasionally for 10 minutes. Add in the garlic and sauté for a couple more minutes.

3. Add in the vegetable broth and the chopped-up cauliflower and bring the heat to a boil.

4. Then, reduce the heat to a simmer and allow the ingredients to cook for 15 minutes or until the cauliflower gets tender.

5. Remove the pot from heat source and proceed to blending it with a hand blender or in a stand-up blender.

6. If using a stand-up blender, be sure to allow the steam to escape occasionally as you blend.

7. Move the soup back into the pot and add in the coconut milk and vinegar. Turn on the heat to low for a while.

8. Serve the soup with some sprinkling of dill and ground pepper. Slurp away!

wwwwwwwwwwwwwwwwwwwwwwwwwwwwwwwwwwwwwwww

Recipe 25: Fennel, Leek and Walnut Soup with Turmeric

There is no coincidence that a walnut nut looks a lot like the brain, considering how it IS brain food! Fennel on the other hand, is great for the upper respiratory tract infections, bronchitis, backaches, and to increase sex drive in women (hint hint). Leek works together with turmeric to give you a double dose of anti-cancer properties and when all the ingredients are put together, you get an out-of-this-world combination of tastes that you simply MUST experience at least once!

Serves: 4-6

Cooking Time: 34 minutes

Ingredients:

- 4 cups of Vegetable Stock
- 4 sprigs of Thyme (leaves), chopped
- 3 Leeks, chopped (use the top greens for stock)
- 2 tbsp. of Grapeseed Oil
- 1 Fennel bulb cored and chopped (save some for garnish!)
- 1 medium Apple, peeled and chopped
- 1 to 2 tsp. of ground Turmeric
- ½ cup of toasted Walnut halves
- Salt and Pepper to taste

Directions:

1. In a large pot, heat the grapeseed oil over medium heat. Add in the chopped thyme and leeks. Let them sauté until they are soft, around 4 minutes.

2. Toss in the fennel and apples. Stir everything for a while before adding in the turmeric. Continue the sautéing process until the fennel is soft (another 4 minutes).

3. Add in the walnuts, season the ingredients with salt and pepper, and add in the vegetable stock.

4. After stirring, bring the ingredients to a boil and simmer for 12 to 15 minutes or until everything is soft.

5. Remove the pot from the heat and blend the ingredients in batches until all is smooth. Bring the soup to a boil once more and determine is the seasoning is sufficient.

6. Serve while it's hot and top it with a dash of black pepper, toasted walnuts, some fennel fronds and a swirl of maple syrup.

wwwwwwwwwwwwwwwwwwwwwwwwwwwwwwwwwwwwwwwww

Recipe 26: Lebanese Semolina Turmeric Cake

Semolina is wonderful when made into a cake. It has got a prominent texture and gives the cake a certain weight in each bite! This recipe is not as sweet as the traditional version of the cake but if sweet is your thing, then feel free to serve with a topping of honey or agave syrup.

Serves: One 9'inch cake

Cooking Time: 45 minutes

Ingredients:

- 1 ½ cups of Semolina Flour
- 1 ⅛ cups of White Sugar
- ½ cup of All-Purpose Flour
- ½ cup of Vegetable Oil
- 1 cup of Milk
- 1 ½ tsp. of Baking Powder
- 1 tsp. of ground Turmeric
- 1 tbsp. of Pine Nuts

Directions:

1. Preheat the oven to 350°F. In a mixing bowl, mix the semolina, flour, baking powder and turmeric.

2. In a larger bowl, add in the milk and sugar, stirring until they are dissolved.

3. Add in the vegetable oil and the flour mixture and beat with an electric beater for 5 minutes at a medium speed.

4. Grease a 9'inch round baking pan. Pour the cake batter into the baking pan and sprinkle pine nuts on the top. Bake for 25 to 35 minutes.

5. Best way to find out if your cake is done, is through poking a toothpick in the center and find no wet pieces of cake stuck on it.

Recipe 27: Blueberry and Turmeric Muffins with Granola on top

Now you can get turmeric in your breakfast muffin as well! The turmeric gives the muffin a beautiful golden color not just on the outside, but on the inside too! Try out this recipe with other berries and nuts if you want, the possibilities are endless really.

Serves: 12 muffins

Cooking Time: 40 minutes

Ingredients:

Dry:

- 1 cup of Rolled Oats
- 1 cup of Walnuts
- 2/3 cup of Buckwheat Flour
- 2 tbsp. of Arrowroot Flour, or substitute with Potato Starch
- 1 tbsp. of Turmeric
- 1 ½ tsp. of Baking Powder
- 1 tsp. of Ground Cinnamon
- ½ tsp. of Baking Soda
- ½ tsp. Sea Salt
- Pinch of Black Pepper

Wet:

- 2/3 cup of Buttermilk
- ⅓ cup of Olive Oil or Butter
- 5 fresh Dates, mashed
- 2 Bananas, mashed
- 3 large Eggs
- A good handful of Blueberries (fresh or frozen)
- Granola Topping:
- ⅓ cup of Rolled Oats
- 1 tbsp. of Honey
- 2 tbsp. Olive Oil or Coconut Oil

Directions:

1. Preheat oven to 400°F. Grease the muffin tray and set aside. First, combine walnuts and rolled oats into a blender or any equipment of choice and blend into a coarse flour.

2. Transfer the ingredients into a large mixing bowl and toss in the rest of the dry ingredients.

3. Then, add in the buttermilk, oil, bananas and dates to the blender and blend until smooth. Mix into the bowl with the dry ingredients.

4. In another bowl, crack the eggs and give them a minute's worth of beating and add them into the bowl as well. Fold the ingredients until they are well combined.

5. Pour the batter into the muffin tins and drop a nice bunch of blueberries on top, giving them a gentle push into the batter.

6. Mix the granola ingredients in a small bowl and sprinkle on top of the muffins. Let the muffins bake for 18 to 20 minutes.

7. Enjoy your freshly baked breakfast muffins!

wwwwwwwwwwwwwwwwwwwwwwwwwwwwwwwwwwwwww

Recipe 28: Turmeric Almond Scones

Made with a combination of three flours, this paleo recipe is definitely good for your body and good tasting too. Carry this delicious snack with you when you're out and about, or stash a few into your children's lunchbox as a treat! Add a scoop of blueberry jam on top to finish it off on a sweet note.

Serves: 6

Cooking Time: 30 minutes

Ingredients:

- 1 ⅓ cup of Almond Flour
- ¼ cup of Arrowroot Flour
- 1 tbsp. of Coconut Flour
- 1 cup of Almonds
- ¼ cup of Red Palm Oil
- 1 tsp. of ground Turmeric
- 1 tsp. of Vanilla Extract
- 3 tbsp. of Maple Syrup
- 1 Egg
- ½ tsp. of Black Pepper
- A pinch of Salt

Directions:

1. Preheat the oven to 350°F.

2. Start by roughly chopping the almonds using a knife or a food processor. Mix the chopped almonds with the almond flour, arrowroot flour, turmeric, black pepper and salt.

3. In another bowl, whisk up the egg, syrup, oil and vanilla extract, and add in the dry ingredients. Mix the ingredients until well combined and it becomes a doughy consistency.

4. Transfer to a cutting board or covered counter top and press the dough down into an inch of thickness. Cut it into sixths.

5. Bake in the oven for 15 to 20 minutes, or until the toothpick comes out with no wet piece stuck to it.

wwwwwwwwwwwwwwwwwwwwwwwwwwwwwwwwwwwwwwww

Recipe 29: Orange, Turmeric and Greek Yoghurt Cake

The orange-yellow color of the cake and the white runny icing of the Greek Yoghurt really look like a combination made for true love. Who cares about over exaggerated cheesecakes and heavily sweetened chocolate cakes when you have this healthier, tasty option to go for!

Serves: 4 servings (2 pieces each)

Cooking Time: 1 hour 15 minutes

Ingredients:

- 1 cup 2 tbsp. of Sugar
- 1 cup 1 tbsp. of Butter
- ½ cup of Greek Yoghurt
- ¾ cup of freshly grated Turmeric
- ¾ cup of Almond Meal
- ½ cup 1 tbsp. of Polenta
- 4 Eggs
- 2 Oranges, zest aside and juiced
- 1 tsp. of Bicarbonate Soda

Icing:

- ½ cup of Greek Yoghurt
- ½ cup of Icing Sugar
- Orange zest for garnishing

Directions:

1. Preheat the oven to 356°F. Line an 8'inch round baking tin with baking paper. Grease it with butter and line the bottom with the polenta.

2. Cream butter and sugar till combined. Add one egg at a time and continue mixing. Add in the turmeric and yoghurt.

3. Fold in the almond meal, polenta and bicarbonate soda. Add in the orange juice and its zest and stir some more.

4. Bake the cake for 1 hour. Once removed from the oven, allow it 5 minutes to cool before turning it over. Let it cool for 1 hour before icing the cake.

5. In order to prepare the icing, take the icing sugar and yoghurt and mix it in a small bowl. Spread the mixture on the cake and use some orange zest as garnish.

wwwwwwwwwwwwwwwwwwwwwwwwwwwwwwwwwwwwwwww

Recipe 30: Turmeric Capsicum Cookies made with Almond Walnut Meal

A flourless and sugarless cookie recipe, this is definitely one recipe that is all about healthiness. Although it may sound strange and unappealing, the cookies reflect the beautiful color and flavors of autumn. It is very easy to make too.

Serves: 6 cookies

Cooking Time: 1 hour 15 minutes

Ingredients:

- 1 cup of Walnut Meal
- ½ cup of Almond Meal
- 1 Red Capsicum
- 3 tbsp. of Coconut Oil
- 1 tsp. of Mixed Herbs
- 2 tsp. of ground Turmeric
- 1 Egg

Directions:

1. Preheat the oven to 356°F. Slice the capsicum and put it on a baking-friendly tray. Toss generously with coconut oil and let it roast for 25 to 30 minutes.

2. Chop the capsicum when it's done.

3. In a mixing bowl, combine the walnut meal, almond meal, mixed herbs, ground turmeric and the chopped capsicum.

4. Whisk the egg separately and add it into the mixture. Continue to stir until ingredients are well integrated.

5. Form the mixture into cookie shapes and lay them on the baking pan.

6. Le it bake in the oven for 20 to 25 minutes, turning the cookie over once at halfway time.

7. Allow cookies to cool before digging into its savory goodness!

wwwwwwwwwwwwwwwwwwwwwwwwwwwwwwwwwwwwwwwww

Conclusion

You did it! Congratulations on cooking your way to the end of this Turmeric Cookbook. Hopefully, you found all 30 of these tasty turmeric recipes easy to follow and delicious! Now, with these 30 Turmeric recipes added to your arsenal of meals, you should be able to mix and match the ingredients to create even other delicious creations that are all tasty and intriguing.

Be sure to leave us a review if you like what you read and that you will join us again for yet another delicious journey.

Until next time… Happy Cooking!

wwwwwwwwwwwwwwwwwwwwwwwwwwwwwwwwwwwwwww

About the Author

Born in New Germantown, Pennsylvania, Stephanie Sharp received a Masters degree from Penn State in English Literature. Driven by her passion to create culinary masterpieces, she applied and was accepted to The International Culinary School of the Art Institute where she excelled in French cuisine. She has married her cooking skills with an aptitude for business by opening her own small cooking school where she teaches students of all ages.

Stephanie's talents extend to being an author as well and she has written over 400 e-books on the art of cooking and baking that include her most popular recipes.

Sharp has been fortunate enough to raise a family near her hometown in Pennsylvania where she, her husband and children live in a beautiful rustic house on an extensive piece of land. Her other passion is taking care of the furry members of her family which include 3 cats, 2 dogs and a potbelly pig named Wilbur.

Watch for more amazing books by Stephanie Sharp coming out in the next few months.

Author's Afterthoughts

I am truly grateful to you for taking the time to read my book. I cherish all of my readers! Thanks ever so much to each of my cherished readers for investing the time to read this book!

With so many options available to you, your choice to buy my book is an honour, so my heartfelt thanks at reading it from beginning to end!

I value your feedback, so please take a moment to submit an honest and open review on Amazon so I can get valuable insight into my readers' opinions and others can benefit from your experience.

Thank you for taking the time to review!

Stephanie Sharp

For announcements about new releases, please

follow my author page on Amazon.com!

(Look for the Follow Bottom under the photo)

You can find that at:

https://www.amazon.com/author/stephanie-sharp

*or Scan **QR-code** below.*

Made in the USA
Monee, IL
12 August 2021

75493106R10062